THE POWER OF HOODOO

Without even touching them, Raymond Tate can suspend a football in mid air, make a polar bear stalk a class of infants and surround an unsuspecting guard with apparently immovable sculptures. Where has his magic power come from and how will it all end? Read on for the amazing adventures of Raymond Tate who lives quite an ordinary life until one day . . .

THE POWER OF HOODOO

Steve Bowles

Illustrated by Elizabeth Wood

Evans Brothers Limited London

First published 1979 by Evans Brothers Limited,
Montague House, Russell Square,
London WCIB 5BX.

British Library Cataloguing in Publication Data

Bowles, Steve
The power of hoodoo. – (Jesters).
I. Title II. Series
823'.9'1J PZ7.B/

ISBN 0-237-45503-X

PRA 6808

Printed and bound in Great Britain
by William Clowes (Beccles) Limited
Beccles and London

Contents

47 Bishops Road,
Linchester,
Essex.
18th October.

Dear Professor Mills,

I saw you on telly the other night asking people to write in and let you know about any strange experiences they'd had which they couldn't explain properly. So I thought I would. It's about this weird power I developed just before the summer holidays – "the fluence" I called it, like in that old Popeye cartoon where Brutus is a hypnotist and he puts Olive Oyl in a trance just by looking her in the eye. I don't expect you to believe what I'm going to tell you but I've got at least one good witness who'll back me up – if you catch him in a good mood and offer him a quid.

We don't learn much at our school so I don't know if there's a proper scientific way to set all this out. In fact, the only lesson where we learn anything at all is English and then it's just how to write stories. And we don't even learn much about that – you'll see why in a minute. Anyway, the only way I'm going to get this lot down is to tell it as if it was a story. Hope you don't mind. Tough if you do. Here goes then . . .

Something Stirred...

First of all, everything seemed normal. I got out of bed, washed, dressed, combed my hair, had breakfast and finally woke up. I looked around my room to see if there was anything I ought to be taking to school but nothing came to mind so off I went. As I say, I didn't feel different at all while I was indoors; it was only when I got outside and was walking down to Tommo's house that I noticed I didn't feel too good. Or, at least, that I felt a bit odd.

Naturally, the first thing I thought of was nipping back home and doing my dying duck act so I could have the day off. Then I had second thoughts. The morning wasn't too good – Art with Scrooge, first two periods (boring), then Maths with Old Man Freeman (AARGH!!) – but that afternoon we were going out with Hart, the teacher who took us for English.

Hart was only a young bloke. He'd come at Easter after our old teacher had left so we hadn't had him long. To tell the truth, he wasn't strict enough to keep us quiet but at least he was better than the old timers who don't know what year it is, let alone what day. We were only going down to the Art Gallery and Museum in South Park for a nose around, but a coach ride with your mates is always a laugh and I didn't want to miss it. It's not often you get out of a prison camp like Red Top Comprehensive. Besides, I didn't feel ill or anything, just a bit peculiar – as if some part of me that I didn't know about was waking up a bit later than the rest of me. And that's just what was happening, only I didn't know about it till I got to Tommo's.

Now Tommo's place is something else. A right show-house. I don't know how he can stand living there, I really don't. Actually, it's not so much the house as his Mum – you've only got to step inside and she sprays you with polish to give you a quick shine. Go in their front door and it smells like school when you come back after the summer holidays. Their hall's got this fancy polished wood floor. I never know whether to step on the mat, risk sliding and cracking my skull or walk on the polish and risk Tommo's Mum cracking it. Either way, it's your life in their hands when you go in his place.

And he's never ready when you get there. I swear if I have Tuesday off, he's still getting ready for the day before when I arrive on Wednesday. It's because his Mum's always tidying things away. In my house everything's all over the place so you can see it all at once. If you keep staring round long enough you're bound to spot what you want to find eventually, but there are so many possible hidey-holes in his mansion, it's hopeless. But you can't have a go at him for being slow because he's just like his Mum – up in the air over the slightest thing. Anyway, that morning wasn't any different in one respect – I had to go in and wait for Tommo as per usual.

I rang the chimes (a bell's not good enough for Tommo's Mum) and he came crashing down the stairs to let me in. "Won't be a sec," he called as he belted back up to his room. Same as usual.

Then Tommo's little sister stuck her nose out of the front-room to see who it was and disaster struck. Their ratty little dog, smelling fresh air and postmen's ankles, slipped round her legs and made a determined escape bid.

Tommo heard him yapping, turned round and yelled, "Hey, catch him! Quick!" (Last time he'd got out it had taken us twenty minutes to collar him and we'd been kept in for being late.)

I made a frantic grab for the hound. But Mrs Tompkins had excelled herself with the polish this time and the mat I was standing on shot out from under my feet. I lost my balance, fell over and, on my way down, whacked this huge and gruesome vase straight off a stupid little table that was standing around just waiting to cause an accident.

Everything went into slow motion in my head like an action replay but I actually froze with horror thinking about the row to come. I remember a great scream of "No!" inside my head but I couldn't work my mouth to make it real. And that's when the vase stopped falling – it just hung there, half way to catastrophe.

I heard Tommo let out an enormous sigh, relief and astonishment all mixed together. For a second or two I still couldn't move. I didn't dare in case I broke whatever spell it was that had saved my bacon. Then, very slowly, I swivelled round and slid across to the vase. Only when I had it in my hands did I breathe out again.

Then it was all go as we straightened everything up before Mrs Tompkins came to see what was happening. The dog had got away in the confusion so I nipped out to see if I could catch him while Tommo recovered and got his things together for school.

It didn't make sense. I couldn't even think about it. The whole thing was so stupid there was nothing to think about: the vase had just stopped in mid air – finish. Not that there was much time for thinking anyway because I had to catch that mangy dog so we could get off to Stalag 13.

I looked around outside but I couldn't see him. "Spot" his name is – trust Mrs T. to go for something original. If he weren't such a sick-making animal you could almost feel sorry for him, the treatment he gets. She has him lying down on a couch all day, if she can, with a dish of best steak all minced up fine and a bowl of peeled grapes for him to dip in his champagne. You'd think the outside world was full of big bad dog butchers all waiting to pounce on poor little Spot the way she keeps him locked up. No wonder he goes berserk when he does get a taste of freedom.

All of a sudden Spot came belting round the corner from the next road as if he'd heard there were free bones down at Tesco. Right behind him came this other mongrel – they were going barmy, having a fantastic time. It didn't take much to see it was odds on that one of them was going to run under the car which was coming along behind and, sure enough, Spot veered off the pavement at the perfect moment for ending it all. I could hardly bear to look, just got ready to shovel up the remains.

But nothing happened – no screech of brakes, no yowl of pain, nothing. The car passed me without any change of pace. It had happened again! Spot was kind of hanging over the edge of the kerb with hardly a paw to stand on. I relaxed, and immediately he started to move again. But I'm not as dumb as I look. Leastways, I must be pretty bright underneath even if it doesn't show very often because, instinctively I suppose, I froze him up again; he wasn't getting away now.

I'm still not sure how I managed to work that one, Prof, because I didn't really know that it was me freezing things up, not properly know, but anyway, freeze him I did. When I got to the spot (oh ho ho!) the other dog was sniffing round very suspiciously and looking as if he wasn't too keen on what his smeller was telling him. I scooped Spot up, whereupon he immediately started squirming and wriggling to get away again but I hung on. Aiming one or two fake kicks at the other hound, I legged it back to Tommo's as quick as I could.

He was just coming out when I got there. "Great!" he said when he saw I'd caught the

prisoner. I just lobbed him into the hall and Tommo slammed the door before he could break out again.

We didn't say anything until we'd got a fair way down the road, we just walked along letting our brains get their breath back. Finally Tommo spat out the big question. "What the hell happened with that vase then?"

"Search me," I said, "but I reckon it's something to do with me because it's just happened again," and I told him all about catching the dog.

When I'd finished he just said, "Strewth!" and then looked blank.

But I'd been thinking a bit by then and there was only one answer which made sense. "Psychokinesis," I said.

"You what?"

"Psychokinesis. You know, some sort of fluence you can put on things with your mind. Like in that book we read with Morris last year, that one about the kids who bent spoons and moved things around just by thinking about them. I reckon that's what I've got, psychokinesis."

"Go on," said Tommo. "Don't be stupid. That's all a con, that rubbish." He can't stand anyone having something he hasn't got.

"Well, it doesn't make sense any other way that I can think of."

"And it don't make sense that way

neither," was all I got back as a reply.

We couldn't argue about it much further then because we'd got to school and the bell had just gone. I suppose that was lucky – argue with Tommo for more than a minute and he's likely to get a bit violent. He's a good mate really, but he's got a terrible temper. We didn't need to say that this wasn't to be mentioned to the others – it wouldn't have taken much to start them off and they'd have been pulling our legs all day.

Anyway, whatever Tommo thought, I could see that this mind-over-matter stuff was the only possible explanation and, to tell the truth, I was feeling a bit chuffed – this could come in dead useful. I might even make a fair bit of money out of it from the telly or the papers. Fame! First thing, though, I had to make sure I could really do it.

I sat down in class and waited for Jacko, our form teacher, to shut everyone up while he did the register. I thought I'd wait for hush so I could really concentrate and give myself a chance – I didn't want to prove myself wrong now; I'd got quite keen on the idea. Finally Jacko got everyone quiet and I looked around for something to work on. On the front desk was a piece of chalk and I thought that for starters I'd just move it from one side to the other. I shut my eyes tight and thought hard for a few seconds – then I took a look.

TIMETABLE

What a shaker! So far as I could tell it hadn't shifted at all. I felt really sick. But I wasn't giving up that easily. I screwed my eyes shut again and had another go. Nothing. I tried nudging Jacko's pen so that he mucked up the register (he goes spare when that happens) but no go. I was really fed up – all my big plans right up the spout.

Then it was assembly. All the way to the hall and all through assembly I kept on trying. I couldn't accept that I wasn't going to become an overnight sensation – it was too good not to be true. But nothing, not so much as a tremor or a twitch did I get from anything I tried to move – not the piano, the potted plants, nor even the fire extinguisher. I was opening and shutting my eyes so much that anyone watching must've thought I'd joined the God Squad overnight and was slipping in a few quick prayers of my own. In desperation I actually tried to slam the door on the headmaster as he went out but it didn't even shiver – which was perhaps just as well, now that I think about it, because he's bad enough to look at without a mangled nose as well. And we'd have had assemblies after school all week because we always get the blame if anything goes wrong.

It wasn't till the beginning of Art that I realized – or thought I realized – what I was doing wrong. Before when I'd done it, it had been an emergency, both times. It was obvious

– I could only do it when I was all het up about something, when I had to prevent a calamity.

Now that I had the answer, I could see it was a doddle proving that I could use my mind to control objects. I went over to the side and got a tray to put the paints in and then got in the queue with Tommo to wait for Scrooge, the Art teacher, who was dishing out the different coloured powders. Going back to my table I decided I'd show them all what a sensation they had in their midst: I got to the middle of the room, shut my eyes and then dropped the tray of paints.

What a mess! I couldn't understand it. I was so sure I'd be able to control something if it really mattered. It took me ages to clear it up. Wouldn't have been so bad if that stupid twit Julian Dobson hadn't slopped all his water amongst it. And I got a clip round the ear from Scrooge before I could tell him it was only an accident – right on the dent that Old Man Freeman had made with his board rubber the day before, too.

"That's the last time I try that lark," I thought as I mopped the floor with a stinking rag that must've been there before Scrooge. "In future I'll leave psychokinesis for the telly."

The Fluence Returns

And so I would have done except that it showed up again all of its own accord without me trying to set it going. (Why? Your guess is as good as mine Prof. Though when I've told you the rest of the story I'll tell you what started the whole thing off.) We were kicking a ball around in the playground at lunch time when it happened. We'd been playing for about ten minutes when one of my mates, Frosty, took an almighty swing at the ball and hammered it straight for the staffroom window. Makes me shudder to think of it, even now. It would have been the end of football in Colditz for about a million years.

Fortunately the old fluence came to our rescue again. In the split second's thought that I managed while the ball was in flight, I could almost feel my mind working on it, turning it aside. The ball made the most amazing swerve you've ever seen, its path bending like a rubber banana. It smashed into the wall with about two inches to spare. It was unreal. But you could almost feel the breeze when everyone breathed again. It was only when I relaxed that I realized how tensed up I'd been. I turned round to see Tommo staring at me, a dirty great question mark in his eyes.

It was then that I found I was able to develop the power in a more scientific way – no more do-or-die efforts. I stood back a little from the game, not really trying to get involved, just making a token effort when the ball came my way so the others wouldn't notice. But I found that, by keeping my eye on the ball and straining myself to do some hard thinking, I could dictate the course of the game more with my mind than with my feet. I gradually learnt how to speed up a pass, slow one down or bend its path so it met our man just right. By the time the game had finished, I had quite a lot of control over the power and we were winning without knocking ourselves out. I was also ready to do a few experiments.

As we went in from the playground I was wondering whether I could only work it on things which were already moving. It didn't take long to check. Watching the crowd carefully to get the timing right, I gave the door into the corridor a mental shove and this kid copped what our beloved headmaster should have got in assembly that morning. The teeth marks are still there, if you want evidence, Prof. Of course, he thought the boy in front had knocked it back at him and by the time I got into the building myself, there was a fair old bundle going on. But, to tell you the truth, I was too keen to get on with my experiments to enjoy it properly and I left them to it.

Now I knew I could shift things that weren't already moving, the next things to find out were how well I could control it and whether the weight of the object I was moving made any difference.

Weight wasn't any problem to test. You have to pass this dirty great aquarium to get from the playground to my form room. (They moan about wasting paper but there's always plenty of money to buy tropical fish and posh armchairs for the teachers.) On your first day at Red Top, some nerks like Jacko tell you that the fish are piranhas and that they use them for

NOTICE
RULES

kids who are late too often. I think they expect you to laugh at that. And they call us "childish"! Anyway, it only took a second when no one was looking to find out I could lift the fish tank in the air, no trouble. And I didn't drop it, neither. It ain't the fishes' fault they're there. So all was going well when I got to my classroom – I just had to suss out what the control mechanism was like.

Jacko let us into the room and we all sat down to wait for him to do the register. While we were hanging about waiting for some dozy girls to get settled I tried the chalk on his desk again and this time I got it rolling about no trouble. I was trying to see how slow I could move it and how fast and then how long it took for the stop signal to get through when Jacko absent-mindedly reached out, picked it up and stuck it in his pocket. He seemed to do it automatically, as if he didn't actually realize what he'd done, but it narked me. Who did he think he was, interfering with my practice?

"Soon have that out of there," I thought – but I was wrong. That was how I found out that I had to be able to see what I was going to move. No pocket-picking – a shame that. I tested it again by trying to pull out the drawing pins holding up the pictures on the back wall but I didn't get anywhere. Still, it was all useful knowledge and, now that I think about it Prof, it might explain why there were so many cock-ups when I was trying to use the power, first of all.

Anyhow, while Jacko did the register I went back to working out how delicate I could be. I'd got my eye on this bit of chalk stuck on the ledge under the blackboard and I thought I'd try to do a picture of Jacko on the board behind his back. It was a bit like using one of those drawing games that look like a telly screen. You twiddle one knob and it makes up and down lines, another knob for side to side lines and both together for a slant or a curve. A bit easier than that, but it still took some doing. I managed a sort of Beano-matchstick-man teacher in the end and then wrote "Jacko is a Wally" by the side of it. The writing was easier than the drawing.

I finished just as Jacko got to the end of the register and he looked as surprised as I felt when I noticed how silent it was. Instead of the usual row that erupts after he calls the last name, everyone was too stunned to speak. They were all staring at the board and I'd been concentrating so hard that I hadn't realized that the others had noticed. Another couple of seconds and Jacko would have clicked on to what was fascinating them and turned around. Then there'd have been a row and a half. Luckily the door opened and this bird walked in, taking everyone's mind off the drawing for a while.

JACKO
IS
A WALLY

We all stayed dead quiet so we could earwig on what she said. We'd seen her around school for a couple of days but we weren't sure who she was yet. Turned out she was a student doing teaching practice and that she was coming down the Art Gallery with us. She'd been sent to sit around and keep an eye on us till Hart had checked that the coach had turned up. Typical, that is. Teachers always give the lousy jobs to the students. Even the beginners like Hart learn that straight off. I suppose when they get really expert at avoiding work, they get made into headmasters.

Anyway, Jacko disappeared back to the staffroom for a quick fag before the first lesson and left us with Miss Nightingale. Almost enough to make us feel sorry for her, a name like that. But if she was too stupid to change it before she started teaching ... well, it's like asking for trouble. She was wearing one of those denim skirts with a big zip down the front – what a challenge!

Everyone had started chatting and fighting and generally ignoring Florence, who was looking a bit uncertain about what to do. She perked up a fraction when Julian Dobson, the class swot, took pity on her and started asking how to spell "floccinaucinihilipilification" and "bdellium" etc. He likes to make people feel at home, does Julian.

Meanwhile, as her attention was else-

where, I went to work on the zip. Only because it was a difficult challenge, of course – I wasn't thinking any further ahead. In fact, it opened up without too much trouble at all, which showed I was really getting the hang of this mind-over-matter stuff.

Unfortunately one of the girls noticed more or less straight away and blurted out "Miss, your zip's undone!" instead of keeping quiet and letting us have a few silent sniggers. Florence turned round to face the blackboard to pull it up but she was doing a fantastic cherry when she turned round again. Bright red, she was. We all held our hands out for a warm and she just stared out of the window, pretending to be fascinated by the litter bushes they grow at our school. I felt a bit sorry for her and so I left the zip alone this time. Well, actually Hart's face appeared at the door, suggesting a different test for my new-found powers.

I was wondering if the force I was exerting from inside my head was equal to what somebody else could produce with their body. To put it simply: if Hart was trying to get in the door, could I hold it shut against him? The quick answer was "Yes". In no time at all, Hart was shoving away then bending down and fiddling with the handle and then shoving again till he was as red in the face as Florence Nightingale had been a few seconds before. Everyone was calling out and egging him on

– "Turn the handle, sir!", "Try the windows!", "Bust it down!" – and we could see him getting madder all the time through the glass. When I finally let go, he came in like Charlie Chaplin, nearly falling flat on his face.

After this, of course, he had to give us a little talk, to show the student that he was the boss. He went on about how we were going to behave while we were out of school. Or, at least, how he hoped we were going to behave. Well, I suppose that's what it was all about – no one ever listens much but that's the sort of thing we usually get before a trip. It makes the teachers happy and you expect to pay something for an afternoon off lessons so we all sat quiet-ish. Except for some of the dimbos up the back who were whistling this old song, "You've got to have Heart", that we used to mess him about with when he first started taking us. The rest of us had given it up weeks before but there's always a few behind the times. Anyway, after a bit we realized that he'd stopped rabbiting and that it was time to go out to the coach.

Rogues' Gallery

Everyone belted down the corridors as fast as they could in order to stake a claim for the back seat. Except for Julian, of course, who was hanging around Florence – the crawler. Probably trying her out on "antidisestablishmentarionism" and "ctenoid" to make her feel better after her embarrassment. Somewhere behind the mob I think I heard Hart calling out for us to walk.

But hurrying didn't do us much good

because the driver was waiting for us on the coach steps to stop any fights – he must have been to our school before. After he'd yelled blue murder for a bit and told us what he'd do if we tried this, that and the other on his nice clean charabanc, Hart puffed up and apologized to him, then told us that if there was any more bad behaviour we wouldn't go at all. They always say that but even a mug like Hart isn't stupid enough to get stuck in a room all afternoon with a class that's been expecting to go out. We stood there quietly, pretending that we were sorry and that we'd be good for the rest of the afternoon. Well, that's the rules, ain't it? When he'd finished, I used the old fluence to turn the emergency handle and shut the driver in the coach's folding door.

It didn't take many threats for Tommo and me to grab the back seat. (Everyone knows Tommo's likely to do something loony when he doesn't get his own way.) The rest of the lads – Frosty and Kev and John – squashed in with us. Straight away Tommo starts whispering to them about my psychokinetic powers and how I'd been the one who'd done the drawing on the board and that. If he can't show off on his own account, he'll do it on somebody else's. They were asking questions as we started off and all the way down to the Art Gallery they were setting little tests like knocking off policemen's helmets or pulling out the bottom

SUPERMART

tin from the stacks of baked beans in the supermarkets we passed. After a bit, even this lot believed me and were ready for some laughs when we got to the Museum. Eventually, the coach pulled into the car park and we all piled out.

We couldn't go in straight away because there was a neat double line of infants following their teacher up the steps and so Hart rounded us up into a muddle to tell us what he wanted us to do when we got inside. He said the infants were probably going to the Museum sections and so it would be best if we looked at the Art first to avoid the crush. There were some statues we ought to look at carefully, he said, because he wanted us to talk about them and give our opinions on modern art in the English lesson the next day. There might be a lot of people inside, he said, and reminded us to be on our best behaviour and that we were representatives of Red Top Comprehensive. Then he led the way up the steps towards the Gallery's revolving doors.

Frosty gave me a nudge and whispered, "Go on!"

Mr Hart wasn't having much luck with doors that particular day but, after his earlier Charlie Chaplin impersonation, the way he went round and round in those revolving ones would definitely have got him a part in films if there'd been some producer watching. Seeing him in trouble again, Florence Nightingale dashed to the rescue. It was so funny watching the pair of them waving their arms and making faces while hopping round in an effort to keep up with the spinning doors that finally I had to let them out because we were laughing so much it hurt.

In the end we all made it into the entrance hall. Hart was giving the doors uneasy glances out of the corner of his eye as he told us to go round in small groups and "DISCUSS" everything we saw, while the old geezer behind the counter where you check in your bags and machine guns was looking very suspiciously at Hart. You could imagine him running for the Sheriff as soon as we were out of sight.

Our mob hung around for a bit pretending to nick the postcards that were on sale so the others could get a start on us. We didn't want too many witnesses when the fun started in case there were awkward questions later. Also I was wondering whether I could move more than one thing at once and was practising by shifting around the bags and coats on the numbered pegs behind the old bloke on guard in the cloakroom. It wasn't very easy and I was knocking myself out with just two at a time, let alone more. Then Tommo said that the next room was more or less clear so we moved on.

It was a gift, that room. A long wide room with blank white walls and a polished wood floor – a bit like a gym without the wall bars. Set out all around it were these dirty great lumps of rock on big wooden stands. They must have weighed about a ton each. Someone had knocked lumps off them here and there and bored holes through them and then polished them up to make statues. They had daft names on them like "Mother and Child" to show you what they were meant to be but they weren't bad really.

Down the far corner of the room was another one of these old blokes in uniform. I suppose he was there to stop people walking off with a statue or two in their pockets but as he wasn't doing much business, he'd nodded off in his chair. We all saw the possibilities straight away and the lads were all so keen to tell me what to do that I thought they'd wake him up. I signalled to them to be quiet and then I got the old fluence working. Very carefully, I lifted one of the statues off the floor and moved it over as near to the old bloke as I could without nudging him awake. Then I set it down. There was a little bump which made him stir and wrinkle his nose, but we all held our breath and luckily he settled back down again. Then I moved the next statue so it stood by the side of the first one.

It only took three or four minutes to surround him completely. There were enough statues to make four complete lines right round

him and I got them close enough together to make it impossible for anyone to squeeze out or in. It was a climbing-only job. Edging the last rock into position, I must have knocked it against one of the other stands because the bloke woke up then. We couldn't see him because we were down at the far end of the room and the statues were really big but we heard these strange snorting and wheezing noises coming from inside the circle as if he knew he'd woken up, yet still thought he was dreaming. We started to wander across the room and he must have heard our footsteps because he called out to us.

"Hey! Help, help! What's been going on? Who's shifted these things? Who's that out there?"

I looked at the others and said in a phoney sort of voice, "Hey lads, that's good, ain't it? Talking rocks. This modern art's a right laugh. How many things do you think they can say?"

"I can't see the speakers," said Tommo. "How do you think it's done?"

By this time the old bloke was bending down and peering through the holes in the statues to see who we were.

"You boys!" he called out. "What you been up to? I'll have the law on you, you'll see. Shift these things back."

"Cor, listen to that," I said. "Not very friendly, these statue things, are they?"

"How do they know we're boys?" asks Tommo in a dim voice. "Rocks don't know boys from old ladies, do they?"

"I'll give you 'old ladies' when I get out of here," hollered the attendant.

"'Ere, listen, they're answering back," said Tommo. "You don't reckon there's a bloke in there, mucking about, do you?"

We all bent down and looked through the holes to see the bloke at the back, all red-faced and angry.

"Yeah, there is, look," I said. "Hey mister, what are you doing in there? How are you going to get out?"

"Look you lot, if you don't move these statues back to the proper places right now, I'll . . . I'll . . ."

"What d'you mean 'move them back'?" Tommo asked him, all innocent. "They must weigh a ton. How could we lift them?"

"Yeah, that's right," the rest of us said in chorus.

"Are you really stuck then, mister?" I said. "Isn't there a door at the back or something?"

"No, there ain't," he bellowed. "And if you didn't move these things, who did? Anyway, don't just stand there like a bunch of lemons, go and get some help."

"Can't you climb out?" I asked. "Over the top, like."

"Of course I can't," he shouted. "These

things are worth hundreds of thousands. I might damage them."

"Hundreds of thousands?" Tommo exclaimed. "Go on. They're only old rocks. Pull the other one."

"I'll pull your neck when I get out of here," hollered the guard.

"Blimey, mister, leave it out. We're only trying to help. No need to get violent. You hang on there and we'll go and see if we can find a crane. Don't go away. Then you can show us how to make statues out of old rocks. There's loads down at Brighton we can use. Make a statue factory and we'll never have to work. See you in an hour or so."

We left him ranting and raving – we had to go, we couldn't keep straight faces any longer. As soon as the door shut, we fell about.

About five minutes later, we'd got over it and gone through into the next room to see what was happening there. It was another room of statues, as it happened, only instead of being big, lumpy stone-and-hole ones, these were spindly metal things – tall, shiny and ticking. You could hear the noises as soon as you went in and it was only after a few seconds that you realized the statues were moving and that this was what was making them tick. All these stainless steel rods were shuffling around each other to make different shapes and the spotlights shining on them made changing patterns as they moved. They were OK – better than the rocks.

The biggest one was in the middle of the room – about twelve feet tall, it must have been, with loads of different rods all clicking around. There were wires connecting up the different parts, like those games little kids play with string on their fingers. It was really smart. But standing in front of it were Hart and Florence Nightingale. He was obviously trying to show off, talking about this statue and waving his arms round in the air to make different shapes. It gets on your nerves when a wet like him acts big and it only needed Kev's suggestion to start me making it a touch more difficult for him to explain.

"Go on, Ray," Kev said. "Stop it moving. Old Hart'll really get his knickers in a twist."

In the end, though, it wasn't Hart's knickers that got twisted. Nor Florence's either. You remember, Prof, how I said I'd had trouble when I was shifting the bags and coats around if I tried to move more than a couple of things at once. Well, I reckon that's where I went wrong here. Because although it was just one statue altogether, the different bits were all moving round independently. It wasn't a case of just saying "Freeze" or something to the whole thing – I had to use the power differently on each part in order to stop them all at once. Unfortunately, I didn't know that at the time.

I suppose it was more like a slow-motion buckle than anything else. The whole thing gradually wrapped itself up into a tangle with accompanying noises – screeches and grindings and squeals – before it sort of bent over to one side and died. You know in those old films when the patient in hospital pours his medicine into the flower vase and all the daisies droop over and wither up – it looked a bit like that, only slower and noisier and more painful.

Hart and Florence just stood there with their mouths wide open, boggling at the wreckage. We took off, sharpish, before they came round and looked for the culprits.

We slowed down again when we got to the Museum part and for a while I didn't muck about at all. They're funny places, museums. If you're ever fed up with hanging around doing nothing and someone says, "Hey, let's go up the museum," everyone groans. Yet, if you do ever get there, you quite enjoy it. They have the stupidest things in there. We wandered round, looking at the different bits of junk, until we came to the section where they have all the nature stuff, animals and birds and so on. And down at the far end of the room was the class of infants we'd seen when we were coming in.

They were standing in front of this big, moth-eaten polar bear that they've got there. It's mounted on its hind legs with its front

paws out so that it looks really huge, especially when you're only little. I can remember being a bit scared of it myself the first time I went down there with my brother when I was about six or seven. The infants' teacher had just finished telling them about it and was moving them on to look at the stuffed birds on the other side of the room. We went over and stood in front of the butterfly display cases.

When the whole class was quiet again, the teacher started talking about the birds in the case they were looking at. I could see one little boy at the back wasn't paying much attention, though. He kept glancing over his shoulder at the polar bear as if he was a bit nervous and didn't like to have it where he couldn't keep an eye on it. Well, I couldn't resist it, could I? I bet you couldn't have either. And it was only a joke.

The next time he looked back towards the teacher, I moved the polar bear about three feet out from the wall. The little kid looked behind him again after a few seconds and his eyes went all round and staring. He turned back to face the front really quickly. Straight away I moved the bear a couple of yards nearer the infants and then left it again.

About a minute later, this little boy takes another peek over his shoulder, obviously hoping that he was imagining it before. He was really shaken when he saw where the bear was

this time – he went white and started nudging the kid next to him. This other boy tried to ignore him, thinking that teacher might tell them off if they didn't pay attention, but in the end he looked round as well and it had the same effect on him as it did on the first one. I waited till they both faced the front again – you could almost see them trembling and my mates were nearly killing themselves to hold back the giggles – and then I moved the bear up till it was only about a yard behind them and we waited till they sneaked another look.

You should have heard the screams! And run! you'd never believe that infants could move that fast. They were out of that room like fleas ditching a soggy cat, with the teacher in hot pursuit. We rolled up.

I don't know if we'd ever have got over the fit if it weren't for the fact that just then this bell started ringing. That stopped us right off. It sounded exactly like the fire alarm at our school. And it smelt like trouble. But there was no way round it. We had to go back to the main entrance and see what was happening even if it did mean we were going to get the chop. And this, Professor, is where the story turns out to have an unhappy ending for both me and you.

Hart Attacks

As we were heading back through the different rooms, we kept bumping into the attendants, all on their feet and with their eyes open. That was an ominous sign and I didn't like the looks they were giving us either – almost as if they knew it was our fault that their tea breaks had been cut short. They were all in groups of two or three, as well, as if they were expecting some kind of attack. "All out; Gallery's closing!" they were calling. We started to walk faster.

When we got to the room with the rock statues, we could see our class up at the end near the door to the main entrance. (The rocks were still bunched together but someone had shunted a few of them around and let the old bloke out.) We walked down to where the others were and hung about at the back. Hart was at the front, looking furious, and Florence was standing next to him, looking at her feet as if she was wondering whether to take up nursing or bus driving. Hart was obviously waiting for everyone to arrive before breaking the good news.

There was a noise coming through the glass doors that led into the entrance hall and, looking through, I could see something like a jumble sale going on. A crowd was arguing with the attendant behind the desk and people were telling him that they'd left an umbrella there and not the fur coat they'd got back or that he'd turned the case full of Top Secret documents they'd parked into a rucksack of mouldy half-eaten sandwiches. Something like that anyway – I couldn't catch the details but they were all pretty mad and I was hoping we'd go out of some back door to avoid them. Somehow I felt as if everyone would know it was all my doing.

Then Hart started yelling and I realized that the last dozy girls must have turned up. For once, we all listened to him.

"Right, you lot. I don't know who's responsible and quite honestly I don't care. I'll leave you to sort that out amongst yourselves. . . ."

(I didn't like the sound of that even though I wasn't sure what was coming next.)

"But since we came here this afternoon, there has been mischief going on the like of which I haven't seen in all the time I've been teaching . . ."

(Which must have been a whole three months!)

"A valuable sculpture has been wrecked, a class of young children scared out of their wits, an attendant has been terrorized and it looks like there's going to be a riot out there in the cloakroom. I don't know how you managed all this and, as I said before, I don't know exactly who's responsible – though I've some very good ideas . . ."

A nasty look came towards our group; we all peered around as if we were trying to spot someone looking guilty.

". . . but I do know that this class has ruined the name of our school and made it extremely unlikely that there'll be any more trips of this kind for a very long time. Well, you needn't think that you're going unpunished. As soon as I get back, I'm going to see the headmaster and discuss it with him. But, in the meanwhile, I've already had a word with the coach driver and told him not to wait for you . . ."

There was a bit of a row at this but Hart kept moaning over the top of it all.

"It's no use complaining about it – the coach has already gone. Miss Nightingale and I will return to school in a taxi and you lot can either walk right back across town or else use some of your ill-deserved pocket money to pay the bus fares. I hope you have a long wait too. And I'm pleased to say that it looks as if it's going to pour with rain any minute."

He said this with an evil half-smile on his face, enjoying the revenge that had been so long coming. It stirred up a lot of shuffling around and muttering. Next to me, I could see Tommo was getting really mad at the thought of arriving back late and soaking wet. He wasn't the only one either; everyone must have been imagining the reception they'd receive at home. But Hart was too worked up to bother.

"What's that, O'Brien?" he said. "You can bring your mother up the school with pleasure and your Granny, too, for all I care. As a class, your behaviour this afternoon has been disgraceful and there aren't any words at all which describe the things one or two of you have done. You'll hear more about this tomorrow, I promise you."

With that he went out, followed by a nervous Miss Nightingale, leaving us all standing there a bit flabbergasted. Action as well as words – from old Hart of all people. He'd managed to out-talk us, too, for once. Amazing. But not amazing enough, because he'd only just disappeared through the door when everyone started looking round for someone to blame. And there was an obvious choice. Me.

I might have guessed that it would be Tommo who'd lead the hunt. If anything goes wrong, he'll never admit that it could be down to him. And talk about tight. Even if he is my mate, I have to admit it. He's so stingy he can peel an orange without taking it out of his pocket. Ask him to spend money to get home when it should have been a free ride – it's a bit like wearing blue and white at Old Trafford. "This is your fault, Taters," he said to me. "You started all this. You can pay my bus fares for a kick off or you'll get duffed."

There was a lot of milling about as people were trying to catch up with the news and my so-called mates were trying to explain it all. Luckily for me, they weren't convincing the others too easily – who'd believe a story like that, after all? – and while they were busy I started to edge over towards the exit. I might have got away quietly but suddenly some quick-witted twit piped up, "Yes, but who was doing it?" and Tommo, getting even madder, hollered back, "Him, you dimbo – Tate!" But when he stuck out his accusing finger, I wasn't on the end of it and he realized I was going, if not quite gone.

"Oi, grab him!" he shouted. "Don't let him get away."

They all surged after me in one big mass, some knowing what they were doing, some just following. But I was through the doors by that time and the fluence came to my rescue, temporarily at least. Actually, it was quite funny to see them hopping up and down on the other side of the glass, tugging away at the handles but getting nowhere. Or, at least, it would have been funny if I'd known that the doors would stay shut even when I took my eyes off them. I backed across the entrance hall, around the edge of the scrum that was still trying to sort hats from coats from parcels, then turned and shot through the revolving doors to the wide world outside.

I belted down the steps and had started across the car park, when I heard this squeaky cry of "Come on!" from my left and, looking round, saw Julian Dobson of all people trying to cut me off. He was whirling his duffle bag round on the end of its string as if he was going to brain me with it. He'd had the intelligence to find a back way out of the building but he was stupid enough to think that the others would follow him. Got carried away by the thought of someone else getting done over for a change, I suppose. He must have imagined the rest of the class were right behind him or he'd never have come charging after me like that, the idiot. Probably read too many stories about Joan of Arc.

All of a sudden, he let go of his duffle bag and it was coming straight at me like a cannon-ball. I only just had time to use my powers to put a swerve on it. It whipped over my head and vanished amongst the branches of a conker tree behind me. Julian suddenly seemed to realize he was on his tod because he screeched to a halt and just stared after his bag. Quickly I fluenced one of those tall, wire mesh litter bins over his head and that kept him quiet for the time being. Which was just as well because now I had to switch the fluence back to holding the revolving doors shut, the rest of the class having battled their way across the crowded entrance hall. Even thumping a weed like Julian might have made me relax my guard for a vital second or two.

I backed away across the tarmac and then over the grass as far as I could, concentrating hard all the time on holding the doors steady. I needed as much of a lead as I could get because, though I'm fairly fast over a short distance, I feel sick if I have to keep it up for very long. Eventually, though, it came down to legging it. And the hunt was on again.

I keep wondering if things would have ended up OK if I'd surrendered right then and

TOWN
PARK
LITTER

coughed up some bus fares. I'll never know.

Even though some of them had given up and gone home, there were still too many enjoying themselves by chasing me for the powers to be of much use. And though it looked like it might pour at any moment, the rain kept off too, more's the pity. I might have got clear if they'd run for shelter. As it was, I headed for the gate on the far side of the park because I thought I might get a bus quicker over that way and get clear before they could close the gap. But before I'd got round the boating lake I could see they were going to catch me. Some went one way round the pond, some the other and, by the time I reached the boat hut, I could see I was going to get pinched between them. So I paid for a boat and headed out on to the lake to sit it out till they got hungry and went off for their tea.

But Tommo's really stubborn when he's mad. He got a canoe and came after me with Frosty. I could still have held them back, of course, but the others were bunging bricks from over the side and I needed all my concentration to make those miss me. With two of them paddling the canoe, it wasn't long before they caught up. I could see I only had one chance. I went as near as I could to the path – on the side opposite the boathouse where all the others were standing and watching. Then I slowed down and let the canoe get right up close. Tommo stood up at the front end, preparing to make a dramatic leap into my boat. I saw him go tense, ready to jump. And then I used the fluence to give the canoe an almighty shove.

He nearly made it – but not quite. I don't think he's forgiven me properly for that even now, though inside he must know that a lot of what happened was his fault. Mind you, that pond is cold and very mucky – I wouldn't fancy swimming in it. Frosty wouldn't let him get near the canoe, either, in case he tipped it over.

Meanwhile, as everyone's attention was stuck on Tommo, I pulled into the side and abandoned ship. I thought I could double back and hide among the trees behind the Gallery. I ran back across the grass towards the car park, looking about carefully in case the rest of the class were lurking in wait. I was just thinking that I'd got clear when something heavy clouted me on the head and I nearly took a nose-dive. I'd forgotten about Julian and the crafty swine had dive-bombed me from the conker tree with his duffle bag.

And, to cut a long story short Prof, that was that. I was a bit dizzy but I staggered on and, in the end, got away from the mob all right. Almost immediately, though, I could tell the powers had gone. At the time I even felt rather glad but looking back I can see that, if I'd had more time to get used to it and hadn't

gone berserk straight away, the old fluence could have been very useful to have around. Course, I've tried tapping my head on walls to see if I can bring it back but no luck so far.

Oh yeah, I remember saying I had an idea about where I got it from, too. Well, working it out backwards from Julian's knock on the napper, I remembered that my favourite teacher – a lovely bloke called Freeman who takes us for Maths – had been trying to fracture my skull with his board rubber the day before when I was talking in his lesson. I decided that's what must have woken up my hidden abilities. I can't make up my mind whether it proves teachers shouldn't hit kids or not.

I got my revenge on Julian, of course, and later on I made it up with Tommo and the lads – though I took a couple of days unofficial holiday from school first to let them get over it. Some of them never saw much, anyway, so it didn't take a lot to convince them I was wrongly accused. And, when you think about it, everything that happened was so weird that even those who were around for a lot of the time find it hard to believe now that it's a few months ago. Give them time and they'll have forgotten all about it. Except Tommo perhaps; every now and again, when he thinks I'm not looking, I catch him staring at me and running his fingers through his hair as if he's cleaning pond-weed out of it.

MATHS

And speaking of Tommo, I'd better get off to see him now. He got on the wrong side of Old Man Freeman today and copped the board rubber treatment. He still felt a bit peculiar when we were coming home tonight so I thought I'd drop in to see him after I'd finished writing this out.

Cheers for now then, Prof. I don't suppose you'll believe all this but maybe you'll hear from somebody else who's had it too and it might make you think. And if I get any signs of it coming back, I'll be in touch.

Yours sincerely,
Raymond Tate.

* * * * *

15 Alexander Road,
Linchester,
Essex.
25th October.

Dear Prof Mills,

You won't know me but my name is Tompkins and . . .

You remind me of a man.
What man?
The man with the power.
What power?
The power of Hoodoo.
Who do?
You do.
Do what?
Remind me of a man.
What man?
The man with the power.
What power?
The power of Hoodoo.
Who do?
You do.
Do what?
Remind me of a man.
What man?
etc.
etc.
etc.